Events
1949

D1359210

News for every
day of the year

Compiled by Hugh Morrison

1949 Oldsmobile 88

Montpelier Publishing
London

Front cover images: Clockwise from left: 1949 Oldsmobile 88, George Orwell, President Truman, RAF English Electric Canberra.

Rear cover images: Clockwise from top: Robert Mitchum, HMS Amethyst, Britain's Chancellor of the Exchequer Sir Stafford Cripps, the Triumph Mayflower, Winston Churchill, Frankie Laine, HRH Princess Elizabeth.

Image credits: Greta Kempton, NBC Radio, Sicnag, J.Fred Henry, *Sporting News*, Waerfelu, Idominick, PD Van Vechten, William Timym, Hugo Van Gelderen/Anefo, University of Cambridge, AK Benson, David Shankbone, Bill Larkins, Afelipe Carvalho, UK Expat, G.Vail, Ash, FORTEPAN/Pál Berkó, Usbotschaft Berlin, Carl Van Vechten, Georges Jansoone, Zonk 43, Ceebeewnz, David Eldan, Cecil Beaton, Bill Ebbesen, Failuresque, Mr Choppers, Deutsche Fotothek/Abraham Pisarek, David Shankbone, Officially Armand Assante, Phil Parker, Steve Nuccia, Raizy/Flominator, Robert LeRoy Knudsen, Gage Skidmore, Alan Light, Carlos Delgado, The World Famous Comedy Store.

ISBN-13: 978-1727810363
ISBN-10: 1727810368

Published by Montpelier Publishing, London.
Printed and distributed by Amazon Createspace.

Events of
1949

**Spencer Tracey and Katharine
Hepburn in *Adam's Rib***

JANUARY 1949

Saturday 1: Peacetime conscription (National Service) is introduced for men aged 18-26 in the United Kingdom.

Sunday 2: Israeli troops withdraw from the Sinai Peninsula, ending the Battles of the Sinai in the Arab-Israeli War.

Monday 3: 37 people are killed by tornadoes in Warren, AR.

Tuesday 4: A UN Security Council committee issues a plan for separate banking systems for East and West Berlin.

Wednesday 5: US President Harry S. Truman gives the annual State of the Union address to congress, proposing his 'Fair Deal' on socio-economic issues.

Thursday 6: Nuri al-Said is re-elected as Prime Minister of Iraq for the fifth time, eventually serving fourteen terms.

Friday 7: One of the world's longest civil wars, the Karen Conflict, begins in Burma.

Saturday 8: *All I Want for Christmas (Is My Two Front Teeth)* by Spike Jones and His Orchestra tops the US Billboard singles chart.

Tommy Handley records *ITMA*.

Sunday 9: British comedian Tommy Handley of popular radio series *ITMA* (*It's That Man Again*) dies aged 56.

JANUARY 1949

Monday 10: RCA Victor announces the 45 rpm microgroove record to compete with Columbia's 33 1/3 rpm version launched in 1948.

Tuesday 11: The US State Department announces it has 'no immediate plans' to comply with communist Hungary's request for the return of its crown jewels, discovered hidden in Austria by the US Army in 1945.

Conductor Arthur Fiedler demonstrates the new 45 rpm records

Wednesday 12: Communist troops close in on Beijing (Peking) and begin shelling the city.

Thursday 13: Israeli and Egyptian representatives begin armistice negotiations on the island of Rhodes.

Friday 14: Poland signs the largest deal of any eastern European country since 1945, providing for an exchange of goods with the UK worth over £260m.

Saturday 15: Three days of the worst race riots in the history of South Africa end with 105 dead.

Sunday 16: Şemsettin Günaltay becomes the eighth Prime Minister of Turkey.

JANUARY 1949

Monday 17: The first Volkswagen Beetle (Bug) arrives in the USA; the cars do not sell and it takes several years before they gain popularity.

Tuesday 18: Industrial designer Philippe Starck born in Paris, France.

Wednesday 19: Singer Robert Palmer (*Addicted to Love*) born in Welwyn Garden City, Hertfordshire (died 2003).

Thursday 20: President Harry S.Truman is inaugurated in Washington, DC *(right)* for a second term. It is the first inauguration to be televised.

Friday 21: Chiang Kai-shek steps down as President of China as Chairman Mao's troops close in.

Saturday 22: Chinese nationalists agree to a peaceful surrender of the capital, Beijing (Peking) to communist forces.

Sunday 23: 'Bozo the Clown' makes his first TV appearance on KTTV Los Angeles.

Chang Kai-shek

JANUARY 1949

Monday 24: Comedian John Belushi (*The Blues Brothers*) is born in Chicago, Illinois (died 1982).

Tuesday 25: The first Emmy Awards (the TV version of the Oscars) is held in Hollywood. *Pantomime Quiz* wins 'Most Popular Television Program'.

Wednesday 26: The Australian Nationality law comes into effect, creating the status of Australian citizen. Prior to this date, Australians were regarded as British subjects in law.

Thursday 27: Hollywood star Tyrone Power marries actress Linda Christian in Rome.

Tyrone Power

Linda Christian

Friday 28: The UN Security Council votes to transfer sovereignty of the Dutch East Indies to a new United States of Indonesia by July 1950.

Saturday 29: Britain grants de facto recognition to the state of Israel.

Sunday 30: Juan Natalicio Gonzalez, President of Paraguay, is overthrown in a coup led by Raimundo Rolon.

JANUARY/FEBRUARY 1949

Monday 31: The serial *These Are My Children* first airs on NBC-TV in the USA, generally credited as the first daytime TV soap opera.

Tuesday 1: The Women's Auxiliary Air Force is renamed the Women's Royal Air Force.

Wednesday 2: Scottish entrepreneur and TV personality Duncan Bannatyne OBE (*Dragon's Den*) born in Clydebank, Scotland.

Thursday 3: US President Harry S.Truman states that he will only negotiate with the USSR via the United Nations.

The Shah of Iran recovers in hospital

Friday 4: An unsuccessful assassination attempt is made on the Shah of Iran, Mohammed Reza Pahlavi, in Tehran.

Oldsmobile 88

Saturday 5: The Soviet Union offers Norway a non-aggression pact if it remains outside NATO.

Sunday 6: The Oldsmobile 88 car is launched in the USA, generally considered to be the first high performance 'muscle car'.

FEBRUARY 1949

Joe DiMaggio

Monday 7: Joe DiMaggio signs a contract with the New York Yankees making him the highest salaried baseball player, rumoured to be paid $90,000 per season.

Tuesday 8: Senior churchman Cardinal Mindszenty is sentenced to life imprisonment in Hungary for opposition to Communist rule.

Wednesday 9: Actor Robert Mitchum receives a 60 day prison sentence in Los Angeles for smoking cannabis.

Thursday 10: Arthur Miller's play *Death of a Salesman* premieres at the Morosco Theatre on Broadway.

Robert Mitchum

Friday 11: Canadian Prime Minister Louis St Laurent arrives in Washington for a three day state visit to discuss US-Canadian relations.

Saturday 12: Hassan al-Banna, founder of the radical Muslim Brotherhood, is assassinated by Egyptian secret agents.

Sunday 13: 15 people are killed in Quito, Ecuador, when crowds panic following the broadcast of a Spanish version of Orson Welles' radio drama, *The War of The Worlds.*

FEBRUARY 1949

Monday 14: US, British and French authorities boycott the opening of Israel's Constituent Assembly over its refusal to recognise the UN's declaration of Jerusalem's international status.

Tuesday 15: The Soviet Union denies allegations that up to 14 million of its citizens are being kept in forced labour camps.

Wednesday 16: The UN Security Council rejects North Korea's application for membership of the United Nations.

Thursday 17: Thailand declares a state of emergency following an influx of communist guerrillas from neighbouring Malaya.

Ezra Pound

Friday 18: An RAF transport plane flies the one millionth ton of supplies into Germany as the Berlin Airlift continues.

Saturday 19: Poet Ezra Pound receives the Bollingen Prize for Poetry. Judges state that Pound's wartime pro-fascism should not distract readers from his objective artistic merit.

Sunday 20: Ivana Trump (*née* Zelníčková), first wife of US President Donald Trump, is born in Zlín, Czechoslovakia.

Ivana Trump

FEBRUARY 1949

Monday 21: Angry protests by Jews occur in the British sector of Berlin following a screening of *Oliver Twist,* due to the film's perceived anti-semitism.

Tuesday 22: Racing driver Niki Lauda born in Vienna, Austria.

Wednesday 23: Mildred Gillars, known as 'Axis Sally', goes on trial for treason following her pro-German radio broadcasts during WW2.

Niki Lauda

Thursday 24: Israeli and Egyptian representatives sign an armistice treaty on the island of Rhodes.

Friday 25: Fifteen Bulgarian protestant churchmen go on trial in Sofia on charges of espionage.

Israeli delegation leader, Walter Eytan, signs the Armistice Agreement between Israel and Egypt.

Saturday 26: The second coup in Paraguay in a month ousts Raimundo Rolón in favour of Felipe Molas López.

Sunday 27: 50 people are killed when fighting breaks out in Thailand following false radio reports of a coup taking place.

FEBRUARY/MARCH 1949

Monday 28: The Australian Broadcasting Company begins its serial *Blue Hills*. It ends in 1976 after 5795 episodes making it at that time the longest serial in radio history.

Tuesday 1: World heavyweight boxing champion Joe Louis announces his retirement.

Joe Louis

Wednesday 2: The USAF B-50 SuperFortress *Lucky Lady II* completes the first non-stop round the world flight, taking 94 hours.

Lucky Lady II during the mid-air refueling required for non-stop flight

Thursday 3: Production of the futuristic Tucker 48 'Torpedo' car ends when the Tucker Corporation closes after stock fraud allegations, later proved baseless.

Friday 4: Israel's application to membership of the United Nations is approved.

Saturday 5: North Korea's leader Kim Il Sung meets with Joseph Stalin in Moscow, securing extensive loans from the USSR.

Sunday 6: The British government announces it is producing plutonium at the Atomic Energy Research Establishment at Harwell, Oxfordshire.

MARCH 1949

Monday 7: Ted Williams signs a contract with the Boston Red Sox for a rumoured $100,000 per annum, making him the highest paid player in baseball.

Tuesday 8: Israeli Prime Minister David Ben-Gurion presents a four year plan for the country, increasing immigration and developing Jerusalem.

Ted Williams

Wednesday 9: In a referendum, New Zealanders vote to allow off-course betting on horse races, illegal in the UK until 1960.

Thursday 10: The romantic film *Little Women* starring June Allyson, Peter Lawford *(left)*, Margaret O'Brien, Elizabeth Taylor and Janet Leigh premieres in New York.

Friday 11: Israel and Transjordan sign a ceasefire agreement similar to that already established with Egypt.

Saturday 12: *Cruising Down the River* by Blue Barron and His Orchestra tops the Billboard singles chart in the US.

Sunday 13: South Korean troops launch an offensive against communist insurgents on the island of Jeju.

MARCH 1949

Monday 14: Wartime clothes rationing ends in the UK, nearly five years after the end of the Second World War.

Tuesday 15: All production restrictions on engineering industries are lifted in British occupied areas of Germany.

Wednesday 16: Actor Erik Estrada (motorcycle cop 'Ponch' Poncherello in *CHiPs*) is born in Harlem, New York.

Clothes rationing poster

Thursday 17: Actor Patrick Duffy (Bobby Ewing in *Dallas*) is born in Townsend, Montana.

Friday 18: Champion snooker player Alex Higgins is born in Belfast, Northern Ireland (died 2010).

Erik Estrada

Saturday 19: Communists in East Germany adopt a constitution to prevent the setting up of a separate West German state after military occupation ends.

Sunday 20: Ten policemen are injured as supporters of Oswald Mosley's Union Movement (for European unity) clash violently with communists in London's East End.

MARCH 1949

Monday 21: Following the previous day's riots in London, the Home Office bans all political marches in the capital for three months.

Tuesday 22: Canada's Finance Minister Douglas Abbott announces major tax cuts from a wide variety of items.

Wednesday 23: The British North American Act 1949 is passed; Newfoundland changes from a British colony to a province of Canada.

Thursday 24: *Hamlet* starring Laurence Olivier wins four Oscars including Best Picture at the 21st Academy Awards in Hollywood.

Laurence Olivier

Friday 25: Operation Priboi begins: the mass deportation of over 90,000 people from the Baltic states to forced settlements in the Soviet Union.

Freight train used to deport Lithuanians during Operation Priboi

Saturday 26: France and Italy sign a trade accord to end tariff duties within a year, and to establish economic union in six years.

Sunday 27: Italy agrees to join NATO.

MARCH/APRIL 1949

Monday 28: British astronomer Fred Hoyle coins the term 'Big Bang' during a talk on BBC radio.

Tuesday 29: *Their Finest Hour*, the second volume in Winston Churchill's epic historical work *The Second World War* is published in the USA.

Husni al-Za'im

Wednesday 30: The government of Syria is overthrown in a bloodless coup led by Husni al-Za'im, Army chief of staff.

Thursday 31: The first RCA-Victor 45 rpm records, announced in January, go on sale in the USA.

Friday 1: Longleat, seat of the Marquess of Bath, becomes the first privately owned historic house in Britain to open to the public.

Saturday 2: All restrictions on electric signs, introduced in Britain to save power during and after the war, are lifted.

Longleat

Sunday 3: Costa Rican government forces quell an attempted coup in the capital, San Jose.

APRIL 1949

Monday 4: The North Atlantic Treaty is signed in Washington, establishing NATO.

Tuesday 5: 69 people are killed in a hospital fire in Effingham, Illinois.

Wednesday 6: Britain's Chancellor of the Exchequer Sir Stafford Cripps makes a £35m surprise increase in taxation.

Milton Berle, host of the first telethon

Thursday 7: The Rodgers and Hammerstein musical, *South Pacific*, opens on Broadway.

Friday 8: The Soviet Union vetoes South Korea's application for admission to the United Nations.

Saturday 9: The first telethon in TV history is broadcast, hosted by comedian Milton Berle. It raises over $1m for the Damon Runyon Memorial Fund for cancer research.

Sunday 10: Golfer Sam Snead wins the Masters Tournament by three strokes, in the first year that the famous Green Jacket is given to the winner.

APRIL 1949

Monday 11: Italy asks the UN to return its pre-war African colonies in order to prepare them for independence.

Tuesday 12: Russian newspaper Pravda accuses the west of sending intelligenc agents to the Turkish-Soviet border posing as archaelogists hunting for Noah's Ark.

Wednesday 13: Eight people are killed and $25m worth of damage is caused when an earthquake hits the towns of Olympia and Tacoma, Washington.

Thursday 14: The last of the Nuremberg Trials of German war criminals by the Allies ends, with 19 people sentenced to imprisonment.

Friday 15: Hollywood actor Wallace Beery (Long John Silver in *Treasure Island*) dies aged 64.

Lt Col Telford Taylor, chief US prosecutor at the final Nuremberg Trials

Saturday 16: The busiest day of the Berlin Airlift: US and British planes fly a record 12,941 tons of supplies into West Berlin during the ongoing Soviet blockade.

Sunday 17: Chinese communists give the Nationalist government until 20 April to agree to surrender terms.

Wallace Beery

APRIL 1949

Monday 18: Éire, formerly the Irish Free State, severs its last links with the United Kingdom as it becomes the Republic of Ireland.

Tuesday 19: US President Harry Truman extends the Marshall Plan of aid to postwar Europe for another 15 months.

Wednesday 20: The Yangtze Incident: 22 men are killed as the British warship HMS *Amethyst*, evacuating British nationals from China, is pinned down by communist artillery fire for ten weeks on the Yangtze River.

HMS *Amethyst*

Thursday 21: The US senate agrees to a slum clearance programme and plans to erect 810,000 public housing units by 1955.

Friday 22: The 1949 Commonwealth Prime Ministers' Conference opens in London.

Saturday 23: Chinese communists capture the province of Nanjing (Nanking).

Sunday 24: Wartime sweet rationing ends in the UK, but is re-introduced four months later due to high demand.

APRIL/MAY 1949

Monday 25: An article in *Look Magazine* predicts that radio will be killed off completely by television in three years.

Tuesday 26: The USSR agrees to end its blockade of West Berlin following the setting of a date for a conference on the future of Germany.

Wednesday 27: The USAF issues an official report on the new phenomenon of 'flying saucers', stating that most of them have a rational explanation.

Thursday 28: The London Declaration is issued, allowing India to remain in the British Commonwealth despite becoming an independent republic.

Friday 29: South Africa's worst rail crash occurs after a signal fails in Orlando, Soweto, killing 74 people.

Gerard Kuiper

Saturday 30: Wolverhampton Wanderers defeat Leicester City 3-1 in the FA Cup Final at Wembley Stadium, London.

Sunday 1: Astronomer Gerard Kuiper discovers Nereid, the second of Neptune's moons.

MAY 1949

Monday 2: Arthur Miller's play *Death of a Salesman* is awarded the Pulitzer Prize for Drama.

Tuesday 3: Chinese communists capture Hangzhou (Hangchow), cutting off Shanghai from the rest of China.

Wednesday 4: The entire Torino football club team is killed when their plane crashes into the Basilica of Superga near Turin, Italy.

Thursday 5: The Council of Europe, a predecessor of the European Union, is formed with ten member states including the United Kingdom.

Friday 6: EDSAC, the first computer with a stored program, goes into operation at Cambridge University.

Saturday 7: The Voice of America and the BBC defeat Soviet efforts to block their broadcasts into the USSR.

Sunday 8: The Soviet War Memorial is unveiled in Treptower Park, Berlin on the fourth anniversary of VE Day.

EDSAC with its designers W. Renwick and M.V. Wilkes

MAY 1949

Billy Joel

Monday 9: Singer Billy Joel is born in the Bronx, New York.

Tuesday 10: Bonn is chosen as the capital of the new West German state, narrowly beating the other contender, Frankfurt.

Wednesday 11: Arab representatives walk out in protest as Israel is admitted as a member of the United Nations.

Thursday 12: The Soviet blockade of Berlin ends after 327 days at 01.46 local time.

Friday 13: The RAF's first jet bomber, the English Electric Canberra makes its first flight.

Saturday 14: *Ghost Riders in the Sky* by Vaughn Monroe and his Orchestra hits number one in the US singles chart.

Canberra bomber

Sunday 15: 25,000 Roman Catholics gather at Ebbet's Field stadium in Brooklyn, NY, to pray for Cardinal József Mindszenty and other clergy imprisoned in communist countries.

MAY 1949

Monday 16: The UN votes to continue its ban on diplomatic relations with General Franco's Spanish government.

Tuesday 17: Newly independent India's Constituent Assembly approves Indian membership of the British Commonwealth, the first republic to do so.

Wednesday 18: Musician Rick Wakeman, keyboard player with Yes, is born in Perivale, Middlesex.

Thursday 19: A record 308 persons are carried by the US Navy flying boat *Caroline Mars*, the world's largest plane at the time.

The Caroline Mars

Friday 20: The US and Britain reject a Russian offer to mediate in the Greek Civil War, stating that involvement must be via the UN.

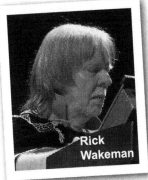

Rick Wakeman

Saturday 21: Violent clashes occur as 16,000 railway workers strike in East Berlin, demanding payment in West German Deutsche Marks.

Sunday 22: 46 people are killed as tornadoes hit the midwest of the USA, including 21 in Cape Girardeau, Missouri.

MAY 1949

Monday 23: The state of West Germany is officially proclaimed in Bonn as Allied occupying forces hand over to civil government led by Konrad Adenaeur.

Tuesday 24: Actor Jim Broadbent (*Harry Potter, Bridget Jones, Paddington*) is born in Lincolnshire, England.

Wednesday 25: Chinese communist forces capture Shanghai.

Thursday 26: British politician Jeremy Corbyn, Labour Party leader, is born in Chippenham, Wiltshire.

Jim Broadbent

Friday 27: Robert Ripley, creator of long running syndicated cartoon *Ripley's Believe It or Not!* dies aged 58.

Communists enter Shanghai

Saturday 28: 52 striking miners are killed in Bolivia as troops are sent in to break the strike.

Sunday 29: The 1st and 2nd British Academy Film Awards are presented in London. Best Picture is awarded to *Odd Man Out* starring James Mason (1947) and *The Fallen Idol* starring Ralph Richardson (1948).

MAY/JUNE 1949

Monday 30: Soviet Foreign Minister Andrey Vyshinsky rejects western proposals for unifying Germany under the West German constitution.

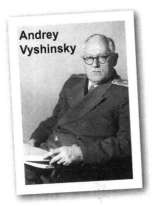

Andrey Vyshinsky

Tuesday 31: Argentina and Britain sign a five year trade treaty.

Wednesday 1: Britain's postwar military governor of Germany, Gen. Sir Brian Robertson is appointed British High Commissioner for West Germany.

British PM Clement Atlee with Gen. Sir Brian Robertson in Berlin.

Thursday 2: Striking Berlin railwaymen reject a compromise by Soviet management and continue their walkout.

Friday 3: Actor Mickey Rooney marries actress Martha Vickers just hours after his divorce to Betty Jane Rase is finalised.

Saturday 4: 'Nimbus' (ridden by Jack Jarvis) wins the Epsom Derby in the first photo-finish in the history of the race.

Sunday 5: Bestselling spy thriller writer Ken Follett (*Eye of the Needle, The Man from St Petersburg*) is born in Cardiff.

JUNE 1949

Monday 6: Sale of alcohol becomes legal in the state of Kansas after 69 years of prohibition.

Tuesday 7: US President Harry S. Truman urges Congress to send $150 of economic aid to South Korea to prevent the spread of communism from the north.

Wednesday 8: George Orwell's prophetic novel *Nineteen Eighty-Four,* predicting a totalitarian society run by the dictator 'Big Brother', is published in the UK.

George Orwell

Thursday 9: US Representative Helen Gagahan Douglas condemns the recent Senate report on Un-American Activities for confusing liberalism with communism.

Friday 10: Car designer Preston Tucker is indicted for fraud in the US, on the grounds of making false claims about his vehicles.

Saturday 11: US and Soviet authorities reach an agreement on the Berlin railway workers'strike, permitting them to receive 60% of pay in West German marks.

Sunday 12: The University of Berkeley, California, requires all faculty members to swear an oath against support for any party or organisation wishing to overthrow the US government.

JUNE 1949

Monday 13: Shakespearian actor Simon Callow CBE *(left)* born in Streatham, London.

Tuesday 14: The rhesus monkey 'Albert II' becomes the first primate in space when he travels to a an altitude of 83 miles in a modified wartime V2 rocket. He is killed when his parachute fails to open on re-entry.

Wednesday 15: Allied forces in West Berlin hand over government to the civil powers, with the exception of security matters.

Thursday 16: The Ealing Comedy film *Whisky Galore* is released in the UK.

Friday 17: The University of Manchester's Manchester Mark One computer sets an industry record by running a program error free for nine hours.

László Rajk

Saturday 18: The Hungarian government announces the arrest of former foreign minister László Rajk and 19 other officials, accusing them of being foreign imperialist agents.

Sunday 19: The first official NASCAR stock car race is held in Charlotte, North Carolina.

JUNE 1949

Monday 20: Singer and record producer Lionel Richie *(left)* born in Tuskegee, Alabama.

Tuesday 21: Ealing Comedy film *Kind Hearts and Coronets* is released. The film stars Alec Guinness, playing nine members of an aristocratic English family.

Wednesday 22: Actress Meryl Streep born in Summit, New Jersey.

Thursday 23: Iran and Iraq sign a treaty of friendship and mutual aid.

Friday 24: The first western TV series, *Hopalong Cassidy,* starring William Boyd, is broadcast in the USA.

William Boyd

Meryl Streep

Saturday 25: Pioneering British geneticist Florence Margaret Durham, a researcher into Mendelian Inheritance, dies aged 80.

Sunday 26: The first general election is held in Belgium since the introduction of women's suffrage.

JUNE/JULY 1949

Monday 27: A seven week long strike by coal miners begins in Australia; it is the first strike to be broken by troops in Australian history.

Tuesday 28: The state of Alabama bans the wearing of masks in public following a spate of disturbances involving the Ku Klux Klan.

Ted Schroeder

Wednesday 29: The US House of Representatives approves President Truman's housing and slum clearance bill.

Thursday 30: The Kingdom of Travancore, a Princely State of the British Empire, becomes part of the Republic of India.

Friday 1: America's Ted Schroeder defeats the Czech Jaroslav Drobny at the Wimbledon Men's tennis final.

Patricia Neal

Saturday 2: The film *The Fountainhead,* based on the Ayn Rand novel of the same name and starring Gary Cooper and Patricia Neal, is released. The film tells the story of a journalist who falls in love with a visionary architect.

Sunday 3: The Yugoslavian government announces it is taking over the economy of the Free Territory of Trieste set up by the allies after WW2.

JULY 1949

Monday 4: Princess Elizabeth (the future Queen Elizabeth II) moves from Buckingham Palace to her first official residence, the nearby Clarence House.

Princess Elizabeth

Tuesday 5: The treason trial of Iva Toguri D'Aquino begins. Known as 'Tokyo Rose', she is accused of broadcasting anti-American propaganda to US forces during WW2.

'Tokyo Rose'

Wednesday 6: Poland joins other eastern European countries in an economic blockade of Yugoslavia over disagreements between Stalin and Yugoslavia's ruler, General Tito.

Thursday 7: British troops unload food on London's waterfront during an unofficial dock workers' strike.

Friday 8: The prohibition of mixed marriages, one of the first pieces of apartheid legislation from South Africa's new National Party, comes into force.

Saturday 9: South African golfer Bobby Locke wins the 78th British Open Championship held at Sandwich, Kent.

Sunday 10: An estimated 7,200 people are killed in an earthquake and landslide in Khait, Tajikistan.

JULY 1949

Monday 11: The German built barque *Pamir,* one of the last of the fast cargo sailing ships, becomes the last commercial sailing ship to round Cape Horn.

The *Pamir*

Tuesday 12: Douglas Hyde, first President of Ireland (1938-1945), dies aged 89.

Wednesday 13: The Vatican warns that all who 'defend and spread' communism will be excommunicated.

Douglas Hyde, first President of Ireland

Thursday 14: Senior American Communist Party member Manning Johnson testifies before the House Un-American Activities Committee, claiming that popular black singer Paul Robeson is a secret communist.

Friday 15: Czech tennis stars Jaroslav Drobný and Vladimír Černík defect to the west during a tournament in Gstaad, Switzerland.

Saturday 16: The Communist Party of Czechoslovakia announces that the church is its 'greatest enemy'.

JULY 1949

Monday 18: The West German film ratings system, set up in conjunction with the allied occupying powers and based on the US Hays Code, goes into effect.

Tuesday 19: France recognises its colony of Laos as an independent state within the French Union.

Wednesday 20: Israel and Syria sign an armistice treaty, agreeing to establish demilitarised zones in disputed territories.

Thursday 21: The US Senate ratifies the North Atlantic Treaty (establishing NATO) by a vote of 82 to 13.

Otto Abetz

Friday 22: A French military court sentences the former German Ambassador to the wartime occupied (Vichy) government, Otto Abetz, to 20 years imprisonment.

Raszyn radio mast

Saturday 23: The Yugoslavian government announces it will withdraw support for Greek communist guerrillas due to their opposition to Yugoslavia's ruler, General Tito.

Sunday 24: The Raszyn radio transmitter mast is completed in Poland. Until 1962 it is Europe's tallest structure at 1099 ft (335m).

JULY 1949

Monday 25: US President Truman asks Congress to provide $1.45 in military aid to the members of NATO.

Tuesday 26: Western allied commanders in Berlin order the restitution of all private property over 1000 Reichsmarks in value which was seized under the Nazi regime.

Wednesday 27: The British de Havilland Comet, the world's first commercial jet airliner, makes its first test flight at Hatfield, Hertfordshire.

de Havilland Comet prototype

Thursday 28: Britain's House of Lords vetoes the government's attempts to nationalise the steel industry, delaying the change until after the next general election.

Friday 29: Britain and the USA announce that the Berlin Airlift will be phased out by 1 October.

Saturday 30: Legal Aid (Public funding for legal representation) is introduced in England and Wales.

Sunday 31: British ship HMS *Amethyst,* held captive by Chinese forces since May, escapes during the night, sending the signal: 'Have rejoined the fleet south of Woosung. No damage. No casualties. God save the King.'

AUGUST 1949

Monday 1: Communists are barred from holding state office in Massachusetts.

Tuesday 2: Britain, France and the USA officially refute accusations from the USSR that the setting up of NATO is a violation of the postwar Italian peace treaty due to concerns over the defence of territory on the Italo-Yugoslavian border.

Peter Wells

Wednesday 3: A ceasefire begins between Dutch and Indonesian nationalist forces in Java and Sumatra after four years of war.

Thursday 4: The head of the US white supremacist group the Ku Klux Klan, 'Grand Wizard' Dr Samuel Green, dies aged 59.

Friday 5: Actress Ingrid Bergman (*Casablanca*) announces her divorce from husband Petter Lindström and her retirement from acting.

Saturday 6: At London's White City stadium Peter Wells sets the English high jump record at 6 ft 5.25 in (1.96m), only to have it broken five minutes later by Ron Pavitt (6 ft 6 in/1.98m).

Sunday 7: A British Gloster Meteor sets a new endurance record for jet aircraft in a 3,600 mile flight over England lasting 12 hours 3 minutes.

AUGUST 1949

Monday 8: Greece, Turkey and Iceland are approved for membership of the Council of Europe.

Tuesday 9: Actor James Stewart *(It's A Wonderful Life)* marries Gloria Hatrick McLean in Hollywood *(left)*.

Wednesday 10: Notorious serial killer John George Haigh, known as the 'acid bath murderer' is hanged at Wandsworth Prison, London.

Thursday 11: The Third Geneva Convention is ratified at a conference of 60 nations, revising agreements on treatment of the wounded, prisoners, and civilians.

Friday 12: In London, Big Ben is slowed down by 4.5 minutes after a large flock of starlings perches on its minute hand.

Saturday 13: 32 people are killed when a Douglas C-47 Skytrain crashes in the Andes en route from Bogota to Ibague.

Sunday 14: The Second World Festival of Youth and Students opens at Újpest Stadium in Budapest, Hungary.

John George Haigh

AUGUST 1949

Monday 15: Nine people are killed and 58 rescued when a Douglas DC-3 air liner en route from Rome to Shannon crashes off the Irish coast.

Tuesday 16: American novelist Margaret Mitchell, author of *Gone with the Wind* dies aged 48.

Wednesday 17: The body of Theodor Herzl, the founder of Zionism, is reburied in Jerusalem. He died in 1904 but specified in his will that his body be reburied should the Jewish state of Israel come into being.

Reburial of Theodore Herzl

Thursday 18: The Soviet Union formally warns the Tito government over the alleged mistreatment of Soviet citizens in Yugoslavia.

Friday 19: 24 people are killed when a BEA Douglas DC-3 air liner crashes on Saddleworth Moor in the north of England.

Saturday 20: The Soviet-aligned Hungarian People's Republic is proclaimed.

Sunday 21: Actress Loretta Devine (*Boston Public, Gray's Anatomy, Everybody Hates Chris*) is born in Houston, Texas.

AUGUST 1949

Monday 22: T.S. Eliot's verse comedy *The Cocktail Party* premieres at the Edinburgh Festival.

Tuesday 23: One of the most senior commanders of the German army (the *Wermacht)*, Field Marshall Erich von Manstein, goes on trial for war crimes in Hamburg.

Larry D.Moore

Wednesday 24: NATO comes into being following French ratification of the North Atlantic Treaty.

Martin Amis

Thursday 25: Novelist Martin Amis (*Time's Arrow, London Fields*), son of author Sir Kingsley Amis, is born in Oxford, England.

Friday 26: Seven sailors are killed when the US submarine Cochino sinks off the coast of Norway following an explosion.

Saturday 27: A concert by civil rights activist Paul Robeson at Peekskill, NY, has to be cancelled when fighting breaks out between opposing factions including communists and the Ku Klux Klan.

Sunday 28: Greek nationalist troops capture Mount Gramos from communist guerillas.

Paul Robeson

AUGUST/SEPTEMBER 1949

Monday 29: The USSR conducts its first nuclear weapons test, exploding its RDS-1 bomb (US codename Joe-1) at Semipalatinsk, Kazakhstan.

Apartheid sign from South Africa

Tuesday 30: Apartheid officially begins in South Africa as the Cape Town post office opens separate white and non-white counters.

Wednesday 31: 16 surviving US Civil War veterans, meet for the 83rd and final gathering of 'The Grand Army of the Republic', in Indianapolis, Indiana.

Thursday 1: Pope Pius XII writes an Apostolic Letter to the church in Poland, commiserating with its suffering under communism.

Joseph Cotten

Friday 2: *The Third Man* starring Orson Welles and Joseph Cotten, with screenplay by Graham Greene, is released. The espionage thriller, set in post-war Vienna, goes on to win the 1949 Grand Prix at the Cannes Film Festival.

Saturday 3: Chinese communist forces capture Xining, the largest city on the Tibetan plateau.

Sunday 4: Further disturbances occur as anti-communist demonstrators clash with leftists at a Paul Robeson concert in Peekskill, NY, postponed from August.

SEPTEMBER 1949

Monday 5: Spain receives its first visit from a monarch in over twenty years as King Abdullah of Jordan arrives for an eleven day tour.

King Abdullah

Tuesday 6: Howard Unruh goes on a shooting rampage in Camden, New Jersey, killing 13 people.

Wednesday 7: The first session of the newly formed West German parliament meets in Bonn.

Thursday 8: Construction begins on the Toronto subway.

Friday 9: 23 people are killed when a bomb explodes on a Canadian Pacific Air Lines flight over Quebec, in the first proven case of mid-air sabotage. Joseph-Albert Guay is later found to have planted the bomb in order to get his wife's life insurance money; he is executed in 1951.

Saturday 10: In a ceremony in Atlantic City, NJ, Jacque Mercer, Miss Arizona, is crowned Miss America 1949.

Sunday 11: Greek war minister Panagiotis Kanellopoulous threatens to attack neighbouring Albania if it continues to harbour Greek guerilla forces.

Kanellopoulous

SEPTEMBER 1949

Monday 12: The UN's Lausanne Conference on the future of the middle east comes to an end.

Tuesday 13: Theodor Heuss becomes the first President of West Germany.

Wednesday 14: New York's governor Thomas E. Dewey orders a grand jury inquiry into the Peekskill riots of the previous month.

Thursday 15: Long running western series *The Lone Ranger* starring Clayton Moore premieres on US TV.

Friday 16: In a Gallup poll, Bob Hope is listed as America's most popular comedian, followed by Milton Berle and Jack Benny.

Clayton Moore as The Lone Ranger

Saturday 17: 118 people are killed when the passenger ship SS *Noronic* catches fire in Toronto Harbour.

Jack Benny (left) and Bob Hope

Sunday 18: As part of the British export drive, Chancellor of the Exchequer Sir Stafford Cripps announces the devaluation of the pound from $4.03 to $2.80.

SEPTEMBER 1949

Twiggy

Monday 19: 1960s British fashion model Twiggy (Lesley Hornby) is born in Neasden, London.

Tuesday 20: Silent film and early 'talkie' star Richard Dix (*The Whistler, The Ghost Ship*) dies aged 56.

Wednesday 21: In Beijing (Peking), Mao Zedong formally announces the establishment of the People's Republic of China.

Bruce Springsteen

Thursday 22: MGM's Oscar-nominated director Sam Wood, who directed the Marx Brothers films *A Night at the Opera* and *A Day at the Races*) dies aged 66.

Friday 23: Singer and songwriter Bruce Springsteen born in Long Branch, New Jersey.

Saturday 24: Chinese communist troops defeat nationalists as the Ningxia Campaign ends.

Sunday 25: Actor Humphrey Bogart is accused of assaulting a woman in a Manhattan nightclub; the charges are later dismissed.

SEPTEMBER/OCTOBER 1949

Monday 26: The first contemporary English translation of Miguel de Cervantes' novel *Don Quixote* by Samuel Putnam, is published.

Tuesday 27: Oklahoma votes to retain prohibition in a special state election; it is the fifth failed attempt to repeal the anti-alcohol law.

Wednesday 28: Britain and Czechoslovakia sign a five year trade pact.

Marshall Tito

Thursday 29: The Soviet Union renounces its former friendship treaty with Yugoslavia as its relations worsen with the country's leader, Marshal Tito.

Friday 30: The Berlin Airlift comes to an end after 277,264 flights delivering 2.3 million tons of supplies since June 1948.

Saturday 1: *That Lucky Old Sun* by Frankie Laine tops the Billboard singles chart in the USA.

Sunday 2: The USSR announces diplomatic recognition of the People's Republic of China and the termination of relations with the former Nationalist government.

Frankie Laine

OCTOBER 1949

Armand Assante

Monday 3: WERD, the first black-owned American radio station, begins broadcasting in Atlanta, Georgia.

Tuesday 4: Actor Armand Assante (*Paradise Alley, The Doctors, Gotti, NCIS*) is born in New York City.

Wednesday 5: Yugoslavia extends diplomatic recognition to the People's Republic of China.

Thursday 6: *The Heiress*, starring Olivia De Havilland, Montgomery Clift and Ralph Richardson premieres in New York.

Friday 7: The Soviet influenced German Democratic Republic (DDR), commonly known as East Germany, is officially established under President Wilhelm Pieck.

Wilhelm Pieck, first President of East Germany

Saturday 8: Actress Sigourney Weaver (*Alien, Working Girl, Avatar*) is born in New York.

Sunday 9: The New York Yankees defeat the Brooklyn Dodgers 10-6 to win the World Series.

Sigourney Weaver

OCTOBER 1949

Monday 10: American pilots Bill Barris and Dick Riedel complete a record non-stop flight of 42 days in a tiny Aeronca Sedan aeroplane. Mid-air refueling was used and food was collected from the ground during low passes.

Tuesday 11: Soviet UN delegate Yakov Malik requests unsuccessfully for member states to release details of their atomic weapons.

Wednesday 12: The last film starring the Marx Brothers, *Love Happy*, premieres in San Francisco.

Thursday 13: Indian Prime Minister Jawaharlal Nehru addresses the US Congress, assuring Americans that India would not remain neutral if 'freedom is menaced'.

Friday 14: After nine months, the Smith Act trial of communist party leaders in the USA ends, with eleven persons found guilty of conspiracy against the US government.

Saturday 15: Chinese communist troops capture Guangzhou (Canton).

Sunday 16: The three and half year long Greek Civil War ends as communist rebels surrender.

Robert Thompson (left) and Benjamin Davis were found guilty of communist conspiracy in the Smith Act trials.

OCTOBER 1949

King Leopold III

Monday 17: Robert A. Heinlein's classic science fiction novel about Martian conquest, *Red Planet* is published.

Tuesday 18: King Leopold III of Belgium, exiled following his capitulation to Germany in 1940, agrees to return to the throne if a referendum supports him.

Wednesday 19: The US completes its final Japanese war crimes trials.

Thursday 20: Seamen in Canada call off their six-and-a half-month-long strike against shipowners.

Benjamin Netanyahu

Friday 21: Benjamin Netanyahu, ninth Prime Minister of Israel, is born in Tel Aviv.

Saturday 22: West Germany's Chancellor, Konrad Adenauer, refuses to recognises the state of East Germany.

Standard Motors Triumph Mayflower

Sunday 23: One of the first British post-war new cars, the Triumph Mayflower, is unveiled.

OCTOBER 1949

Monday 24: The cornerstone of the permanent headquarters of the United Nations is laid in New York City.

Tuesday 25: A British de Havilland Comet flown by Wing Commander John Cunningham flies from London to Tripoli and back in a record 6 hours 38 minutes.

Wednesday 26: The Fair Labor Standards Amendment of 1949 raises the US minimum wage from 40 to 75 cents per hour.

John Cunningham

Thursday 27: Chinese communists lose the Battle of Guningtou, failing to take the island of Taiwan from nationalist forces. As a result, Taiwan remains the last stronghold of the pre-revolutionary Republic of China to the present day.

Friday 28: Eugenie Anderson becomes the first female US ambassador when she is appointed envoy to Denmark.

Saturday 29: James Graham, 6th Duke of Montrose, becomes the first of 600 signatories to a petition demanding home rule for Scotland under the British crown.

Sunday 30: Historical novel *The Egyptian* by Finnish author Mika Waltari tops the *New York Times* bestseller list, where it remains for 16 weeks.

Mika Waltari

OCTOBER/NOVEMBER 1949

Monday 31: The Guangxi Campaign of the Chinese Civil War begins.

Tuesday 1: 55 people are killed when an Eastern Airlines Douglas DC-4 crashes en route from Boston to Washington DC, the worst aviation disaster in US history to that date.

Wednesday 2: 19 year old Princess Margaret, sister of HM Queen Elizabeth II, is seen smoking a cigarette at a charity ball, the first member of the royal family to smoke at a public event.

HRH Princess Margaret

Thursday 3: Businessman and art collector Solomon R. Guggenheim, dies aged 88. His collection forms the basis of the Guggenheim Museum, New York.

Friday 4: The UN proposes an arms embargo against Bulgaria and Albania, to prevent them aiding communists in Greece.

Saturday 5: In China, the Battle of Dengbu Island ends in a nationalist victory.

Sunday 6: 70 miners are killed in an explosion at a uranium mine near Zwickau, East Germany.

Interior of New York's Guggenheim Museum

NOVEMBER 1949

Monday 7: The first meeting of the Council of Europe is held in Strasbourg, France.

Tuesday 8: Film noir drama *All the King's Men* starring Broderick Crawford premieres in New York City.

Wednesday 9: East Germany restores full civil rights to former Nazi party members not convicted of war crimes.

Thursday 10: Ann Reinking, dancer and choreographer (*Chicago, Sweet Charity, Annie*) is born in Seattle, Washington.

VW Type 2

Friday 11: A nationwide strike by the United Steelworkers of the USA ends in agreement with the US Steel Corporation.

Saturday 12: The Volkswagen Type 2 camper van or 'combi' is unveiled to the public.

Sunday 13: Antonio de Oliveira Salazar, dictator of Portugal, is re-elected in elections criticised by some opposition parties as undemocratic.

Portugal's Antonio de Oliveira Salazar

NOVEMBER 1949

Monday 14: The Polish Communist Party expels three ex-leaders, on grounds of disloyalty to the party line.

Tuesday 15: British boxer Eddie Vann sets a new record for the fastest knockout in a heavyweight boxing match, when his opponent George Stern goes down after 12 seconds in the first round.

Wednesday 16: Students in Ghent, Belgium, storm the town's medieval castle and throw fruit from the walls onto police in protest at a new tax on beer.

Thursday 17: The communist-leaning Women's International Democratic Federation meets in Moscow with delegates from 46 countries.

Friday 18: The romantic comedy film *Adam's Rib* starring Spencer Tracy and Katherine Hepburn *(right)* is released.

Rainier III

Saturday 19: The coronation takes place of Prince Rainier III of Monaco.

Sunday 20: Faced with the prospect of a military coup, Panamanian President Daniel Chanis Pinzón resigns in favour of Vice President Roberto Chiari.

NOVEMBER 1949

Monday 21: The UN approves a compromise on governance of former Italian colonies, granting independence to Libya by 1952 and Italian Somaliland by 1959.

Tuesday 22: As part of the Paris Plan, the US, Britain and France lift many of their postwar economic and diplomatic restrictions on West Germany.

Wednesday 23: Gujarat University is established at Ahmedabad, India.

Thursday 24: In a bitterly contested vote, the House of Lords approves the nationalisation of the British iron and steel industry by 1 January 1951.

Friday 25: A one day general strike takes place in France over pay levels.

Saturday 26: Frankie Laine knocks his own song off the top of the US charts, as *Mule Train* replaces *That Lucky Old Sun* at number one.

Globemaster II

Sunday 27: The Douglas C-124 *Globemaster II,* the primary transport plane for the USAF in the 50s and 60s, makes its first flight.

NOVEMBER/DECEMBER 1949

Monday 28: In a speech at London's Kingsway Hall, former Prime Minister Winston Churchill proposes discussion on closer co-operation between Britain and Europe.

Tuesday 29: Comedian, writer and actor Gary Shandling is born in Chicago, Illinois (died 2016).

Garry Shandling

Wednesday 30: Chinese communist forces capture Chongqing (Chunking).

Thursday 1: Notorious drug smuggler Pablo Escobar is born in Rionegro, Colombia (died 1993).

Friday 2: The US State Department officially warns the Chinese nationalist government over its shelling of the merchant ship *Sir John Franklin* in the Yangtze River.

Jeff Bridges

Saturday 3: A Congressional investigation is ordered into allegations that one of President Roosevelt's advisors, the late Harry Hopkins, gave atomic secrets to the Soviets.

Sunday 4: Actor Jeff Bridges (*Iron Man, The Big Lebowski, The Fabulous Baker Boys*) is born in Los Angeles, California.

DECEMBER 1949

Monday 5: Composer Arturo Toscanini is made a lifetime senator of the Italian Republic for services to music.

Tuesday 6: US blues/folk artist Lead Belly dies aged 61.

Lead Belly

Wednesday 7: Leslie Groves, director of the wartime US atomic weapons research, tells the House Un-American Activities Committee that Russian spies were operating in US laboratories during WW2.

Thursday 8: The musical film *On the Town* starring Gene Kelly, Frank Sinatra, Betty Garrett and Ann Miller is released.

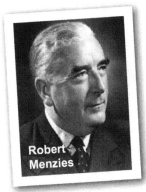

Robert Menzies

Friday 9: East Germany announces that the Christmas holiday will be banned and any religious celebrations discouraged.

Saturday 10: Robert Menzie's Liberal Party is victorious in Australia's federal elections, defeating Ben Chifley's Labor Party.

Sunday 11: The 'Číhošť miracle' is alleged to have taken place at a church in Czechoslovakia. Parishioners reported a large cross moving several times of its own accord. Secret police force the priest, Josef Toufar, to confess that he faked the incident; he dies soon afterwards most likely of injuries sustained while under interrogation.

DECEMBER 1949

Bill Nighy

Monday 12: Actor Bill Nighy (*Love Actually, The Best Exotic Marigold Hotel*) is born in Caterham, Surrey, England.

Tuesday 13: The Israeli government moves from Tel Aviv to Jerusalem.

Wednesday 14: War film *The Sands of Iwo Jima,* starring John Wayne, premieres in San Francisco.

Thursday 15: The famous 'Birdland' jazz club opens on 1678 Broadway, New York. The opening night performers include Lester Young, Charlie Parker and Harry Belafonte.

Friday 16: The Parliament Act 1949 removes the right of the British upper chamber, the House of Lords, from vetoing legislation from the House of Commons.

John Wayne in *The Sands of Iwo Jima*

Saturday 17: The Sutton Coldfield transmitting station begins BBC TV broadcasts to the English Midlands, the first TV service outside London.

Sunday 18: The Philadelphia Eagles defeat the Los Angeles Rams 14-0 in the 1949 NFL Championship Game in Los Angeles.

DECEMBER 1949

Monday 19: The trial of Field Marshall Erich von Manstein ends; he is sentenced to 18 years' imprisonment for war crimes; (released in 1953 on health grounds).

Tuesday 20: Actor Clark Gable marries Sylvia Ashley in Solvang, California *(right)*. It is the fourth marriage for both of them.

Wednesday 21: Joseph Stalin is awarded the Order of Lenin as part of the celebrations for his 70th birthday.

Thursday 22: Twin brothers Maurice and Robin Gibb of the Bee Gees are born in Douglas, Isle of Man (died 2003 and 2012 respectively).

Friday 23: Pope Pius XII invites all Protestants and Jews to return to the 'one true church' in union against militant atheism.

Cary Grant and Betsy Drake

Saturday 24: At least 86 civilians are killed by troops in Mungyeong, South Korea, during a clampdown on communists.

Sunday 25: Actor Cary Grant marries Betsy Drake in Phoenix, Arizona: aviation magnate Howard Hughes is best man.

DECEMBER 1949

Monday 26: Albert Einstein publishes his *Generalized Theory of Gravitation.*

Tuesday 27: In a ceremony in Amsterdam, Queen Juliana of the Netherlands transfers Dutch sovereignty over Indonesia.

Winston Churchill

Wednesday 28: *Time* magazine announces that Winston Churchill has been chosen as 'man of the half century'.

Thursday 29: The Hungarian government orders the nationalisation of all remaining private industry.

Friday 30: Prince Leopold IV, last ruler of the tiny independent European principality of Lippe (ceded to West Germany in 1947), dies aged 78.

Saturday 31: London's Big Ben is shown striking midnight live on BBC TV for the first time, a tradition that has continued ever since.

Queen Juliana of the Netherlands formally grants independence to the Dutch colony of Indonesia

BIRTHDAY NOTEBOOKS

FROM
MONTPELIER PUBLISHING

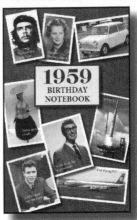

Handy 60-page ruled notebooks with a significant event of the year on each page.

A great alternative to a birthday card.
Available from Amazon.

Made in the USA
San Bernardino, CA
25 February 2019